Snuggle Up,

ZooBorns!

by Andrew Bleiman and Chris Eastland

Most of the photos in this book were previously published in
ZooBorns, ZooBorns: The Next Generation, and *ZooBorns: Motherly Love.*

Ready-to-Read

Simon Spotlight
New York London Toronto Sydney New Delhi

SIMON SPOTLIGHT
An imprint of Simon & Schuster Children's Publishing Division
1230 Avenue of the Americas, New York, New York 10020
This Simon Spotlight edition September 2015
Most of the photos in this book were previously published in *ZooBorns*,
ZooBorns: The Next Generation, and *ZooBorns: Motherly Love*.
Text copyright © 2015 by ZooBorns LLC
Photos copyright © 2010, 2012, 2015 by ZooBorns LLC
All rights reserved, including the right of reproduction in whole or in part in any form.
SIMON SPOTLIGHT, READY-TO-READ, and colophon are registered trademarks of Simon & Schuster, Inc.
For information about special discounts for bulk purchases, please contact Simon & Schuster Special Sales
at 1-866-506-1949 or business@simonandschuster.com.
Manufactured in the United States of America 0815 LAK
10 9 8 7 6 5 4 3 2 1
This book has been cataloged with the Library of Congress.
ISBN 978-1-4814-3101-9 (hc)
ISBN 978-1-4814-3100-2 (pbk)
ISBN 978-1-4814-3102-6 (eBook)

Welcome to the wonderful world of
ZooBorns!

The newborn animals featured in this book live
in zoos around the world. Get to know them through
adorable photos and fun facts written in language that
is just right for emerging readers. Your child might not
be able to pronounce all the animal species names yet,
but if you stay close by, you can help sound them out.

This book can also be used as a tool to begin a
conversation about endangered species. The more
we learn about animals in zoos, the more we can do
to protect animals in the wild. Please visit your
local accredited zoo or aquarium to learn more!

This baby koala
is ready for a nap.
Koalas sleep for
eighteen hours a day!

Snuggle up, baby koala!

Polar bears, like Arktos
and his mom,
live in the Arctic.
It is a cold place to live!

Snuggle up, baby polar bear!

These four baby meerkats
are brothers and sisters.
They do everything
together!

Snuggle up, baby meerkats!

Rooby is a baby kangaroo. She lives in a fluffy, warm pouch until she gets bigger.

Snuggle up, baby kangaroo!

Snow leopards live
high up in the mountains.
Their fur keeps them warm
on chilly days.

Snuggle up, baby snow leopard!

This baby orangutan loves to hug his mom. He holds on to her when she swings from tree to tree.

Snuggle up, baby orangutan!

These baby lions
cuddle with their mom
after a long day
of play.

Snuggle up, baby lions!

The tiny java mousedeer is among the world's smallest hoofed mammals. Fully grown, they weigh less than four pounds.

Snuggle up, baby java mousedeer!

This flamingo
tucks her baby
under her wing
to keep him safe.

Snuggle up, baby flamingo!

This baby tiger knows
that the best thing of all
is a hug from his mom.

Snuggle up, baby tiger!

Special thanks to the photographers and institutions that made ZooBorns! possible:

Cover:
KOALA
Richard Rokes/Riverbanks Zoo
and Garden

KOALA
Jonas Verhulst/Planckendael, Taronga Zoo

POLAR BEAR
Arktos
Daniel Zupanc/Zoo Vienna

MEERKATS
Seth Bynam/Point Defiance Zoo
and Aquarium

KANGAROO
Rooby
Darlene Stack/Assiniboine Park Zoo

SNOW LEOPARD
Emmanuel Keller/Zoo Basel

ORANGUTAN
Tatau and Mali
Ray Wiltshire/Paignton Zoo

LIONS
Ryan Hawk/Woodland Park Zoo

JAVA MOUSEDEER
Lumi
Daniel Zupanc/Zurich Zoo

FLAMINGO
Dennis Dow/Woodland Park Zoo

TIGER
Bahagia and CJ
Eric Bowker/Sacramento Zoo